Ecologia is truly a study of the home, equally comfortable exploring the room of the body as it is exploring the room of the mind, though the speaker resides in uncomfortable liminality. This first collection of poems by Tonnessen holds a Heraclitan tension on the topic of transition. From shifts of body, to shifts of love, to shifts of work, from shifts of diction and syntax, from shifts of lyricism to the more linear, this collection culminates them eruditely and with inspiring grace.

David Tomas Martinez, Poet and author of *Hustle* and *Post Traumatic Hood Disorder*

With earnestness and urgency, *Ecologia* chronicles a transformation, a translation of energy and spirit within the force and fragility of the physical body. The poems process this energy with the momentum of the natural world — a storm surge, a dazed sparrow, *a shadow passing over long grasses.* Tonnessen does not spare us the brutality of rebirth but allows relief in detailing the humor, the eroticism, and the ordinary, delicate beauty of this life. This book reminds us of what it is to inhabit a body, to live with uncertainty, to hurt and to heal, and it resonates with the humble magic of resilience: *And the grace in falling too, as rain comes to rescue. / How many times have I been buried, and come back again?*

Carey McHugh, Poet and author of *American Gramophone*

Previous Praise for Sophia Anfinn Tonnessen's *Ecologia*

Tonnessen's poems examine transitions and transformations in all their danger and beauty ... [Her] sprawling poems often employ pauses or unfinished lines, sometimes to convey wry or fraught understatement. The speaker works her way from anguish to a deeply felt sense of spiritual union ... and continually achieves lyrical moments of grace that feel utterly authentic, making these seeming dislocations into a connected whole and a beautiful manifestation of her experiences. A well-crafted, tender collection that emphasizes exploration.

Kirkus Reviews, Starred Review

Sophia Anfinn Tonnessen's debut collection, *Ecologia,* is a wild ride, its wildness built on joy and anger and desire and I'll-have-no-more-of-this-ness ... Tonnessen reaches all the way for the blue divine — and gets there. The poems most strikingly collapse the gap between map and world, between word and thing, between desire and the having of it ... *Ecologia* reminds me that a basic structure of desire is the mapping of thoughts and wishes into our bodies, and that such mapping changes everything: wish and memory, movement and body, dream and name.

Ezra Dan Feldman, *Gertrude*

An astounding debut, Sophia Anfinn Tonnessen's *Ecologia* is a new trans theology rooted in the natural world ... The poet makes known that she is writing after thousands of years of poetic, christian tradition, white western tradition. Every poem is the result of every poem that came before it; *Ecologia* does not shy away from this ... There's no room for shame in this book, or rather, through poetry, the poet is able to chase it away ... *Ecologia* is what blooms forth.

SG Huerta, *manywor(l)ds*

With passion and precision, ardor and humor, Whitmanian exuberance and Dickinsonian canniness, Sophia Anfinn Tonnessen's *Ecologia* springs up from the "wounded place" that is also "holy ground." I don't know when I've read a debut collection with such panache and such depth. Tracking the poet's transition, this book discovers tremendous vitality in its gorgeous and invigorating openness to change. Here's an entirely original contribution to the mosaic of American poetry.

Peter Campion, Poet and critic, and author of *One Summer Evening at the Falls* and *Radical as Reality: Form and Freedom in American Poetry,* among other collections

Choke

Choke Sophia

Anfinn Tonnessen

Atlanta

FIRST EDITION

Printed in the United States of America

LIBRARY OF CONGRESS RECORD

Name: Tonnessen, Sophia Anfinn 1996 — author.
Title: Choke / Sophia Anfinn .
Edition: First edition.
Published: Atlanta : Unbound Edition Press, 2024.

LCCN: 2024937419
LCCN Permalink: https://lccn.loc.gov/2023934946
ISBN: 979-8-9906141-0-9 (fine softcover)

Designed by Eleanor Safe and Joseph Floresca
Printed by Bookmobile, Minneapolis, MN
Distributed by Itasca Books

123456789

Unbound Edition Press
1270 Caroline Street, Suite D120
Box 448
Atlanta, GA 30307

for Juniper —
beloved, home, and balm

Contents

MILK

Choke

The objectivity of our conclusions is indisputable; however, it was obvious to us, even before we began our research on the psychology of the transgender subject, that the subject's understanding of itself was delusional, unfounded, and perverse in the extreme. No one could blame us if we started our work with a twist of revulsion in our hearts, especially given that our project is one of compassion: to cure the transgender subject of what makes it so profoundly unhappy; of proving that there is no such thing, no disease, state of mind or body, that makes one transgender other than one's own unhealth – and pathological insistence on such.

What follows is proof: a documentation of the subject, studied in microcosm, through her own attempts to communicate experience, emotion, and self through writings, accompanied by field notes, photographs, and a few interventions of our own. It self-selected, coming to us asking to be cured, which in other circumstances would disqualify it – but in this particular case, it was useful to us to have a subject so willing to expose itself.

We do not wish to delve into sentiment, to be inefficient or irrational in our use of time and the funding (graciously accepted) by our patrons in support of the project. We did, a few among us, at least, find the subject a fascinating animal: poking it with needles, calling it 'he' or 'she' to test different reactions, exposing it to a variety of circumstances and information to determine what it might endure. Sometimes it went headlong into violence; other times, it curled up on the couch and failed to respond to stimuli, no matter what we showed it. Our fascination did not extend to understanding. The transgender delusion is one which is destroying its subject, more and more each day it attempts to live in the world.

RUIN

White Shirt Neat Hair

I remember my murderer.   A bitter cousin
chops, tosses me
bright with bleed (as maple leaves)
to dogs choking at their collars.
Mine, my father smothering
a woman.   Do it: I insist.
Bury me in your very body.
Allow me to live, until.

Then — on an ambivalent November day
(caught unawares)   I'll leap the feeble bridges of your ribs,
harpoon the whaling of your belly
& burst redswell within.
Tear your gut with petals soft as veal.
Birth me —
you have no choice.

I am a wine fermented in you. I eschew
headline martyrdom, the search for a missing body —
stay with me, you'll know the meaning of missing bodies.
I bloom algae's green,
outward, upward —
my work is turning your children to my tides,
sowing some tenderness, some liberation in them.

You are what you deny.
A handful of pomegranate seeds
defy, but can't delay, the spring's rush –
those redded eyes that run – let me run
back to the beginning. Let me die unfinished.
My body fed on sagelands, sagelands soiled by me.
Decompose, compress to coal, the dull stone of bone,
I am dust throughout thinned troposphere,
spores in your glassy heart –
that greenhouse, overgrown with choke.

It Takes Two

Second variation on my death:
When I'm at Eight Ball, a (cis) man flirts (super straight! God
    blesses) –
his mistake – gags on skirt and eyeliner. Making him want.
Flutter I, a crush of bass, in nets, defenseless.

My date begins to nod off as I speak (Cassandra) on the present
    crisis - women's sports, HRT bans, somehow, chess,
    HB 4075, another unreported death,
years spent before the first of many gates –
yeah, I believe you, but I've heard it all before –
He's more interested in the follow-ups:
Are you pre-op or post-op?   *Sorry, I'm looking for a female.*
Will you top me?   *I've just gotten into trans girls.*
        I am mid combat op, thank you,
        about to dissolve my target with a splash of Natty Light
        Yes. Spread wide.
        We're all rage.

Who will buy me another drink,
under cover of night take my pussy racing,
slide a knifish cock inside me
splendid, bred?
Will your sexts be poetic, lyric, Shakespearian?
– or better yet, quotes from other authors, since you have never
    cut it.

You know, I don't want to meet your mother yet.
Ask her for me — any 29yo, 6'2", wellhung dom who'd like
to be the bearer of my seed?   No strings.
Any truck driver,
financier, literally guaranteed to make me cum?

At home, I say, I had a grand old time.   I didn't oh
I do cultivate my fear, gnaw paranoia,   spit and swirl;
is it easier to live as Sophia here, than in your home country?
Oh sweetie. Sweet child.   This is my home country,
I am empress-not-yet-exiled, creating crowns
from whatever drifted to the beach beside me-
twigs, garotte, coral, twine,
bikini tops.   I've done it all my life.
            This is my home country.   Too familiar is her ruin.
            I feel heaven like a wet flame,
            spreading up me: my body is a sword
            you've said -

Come to sea instead of fire: these slim wedding-white veils
      of foam,
the healthy heat of my coral-cuts and burns,
consider starting a spiritual journey.
Join the bruselki,   suchki, tanned unevenly,
(your fear's appalling, really, darling - breathe).

I'll leave it up to you what makes my mark:
these lips on your thigh (unshaved),
misbehavior, questioning, a bad pun
under streetlights (high before I fall asleep).
I'll leave it to the sea, to you.
I am giving up my possessions, injections,
prescriptions of who to fear and who to die for,
heading further south and still   I came back here.

Beware me. Beware.
I rise like mermaid voices from water to the air,
name, finger, collect you
to repurpose you for wickedness.
Temptation is my middle name.
Temptation is my vice, my grin
at something undeniable.

I am yours,   ragdoll,
warrior, bimbo, plaything, trying not to make eye contact
in the women's bathroom –
after taking booty pics, get your fix of me,
catch fire with want for me.
My second dying its own style of desire,
pulling you deep, & further in.

r/GenderCritical

I approach you. Looking down, and skylarks.
I am nebulous. No one
pins me down, adds to history's sprawling list of lost causes.
Stage Whisper: *Change pitch, suck in, dewy eyes, meet gaze.*
Even if you are convinced. Even if I choke –
is it supposed to taste like this?

Let me explain –

start, maybe, with grated ginger, warm bitterness's purge,
then follow me through pain's blunt gamut –
does it matter to you what my body's been called?
after all, what's in a name? *would a rose by any other, etc.*
Some bodies call this feeling
dysphoria. Don't know her, does she even go here?

When it comes down to me and the children, I want what's best.
And what's best is never knowing
what we never knew. Not testing
any limits. Breaking any body.
Not to bite it, bash it, bruise it.
Use it up. Use me up.
Yes, I forgot to shave today. No, I didn't sleep okay.
I left peace of mind behind,
totally wrecked the vibes. *Uwu,*

daddy, leave me ruined. I get trenching-deep.
And skylarks.
Modify my body.
Don't ask a third time. I'm already ready, really. Titties out.
Get you in trouble, the feminists too. Set back
a century or two, thanks to these girldicks.
Third time's the charm.

You're in danger-
from a vampire endangering
cis women walking by.
I could devour them, I would. I do.
Let me apologize -
you should fear
me: that I want to wear the years
stolen from me. Passing as perfect
innocence.
Tranny.
TIM. Buy these slurs now! —
Taste the murky, uncertain gold of ginger.
To serve with tongue in cheek.
Slay, girl, with thy libel, your impeccable fit.
With your god-given
cunt.
So you fear me — hysterical, in harmony, you cream for me.

You epiphany. Hairy hands,
cracked lip,   ripped jeans. It's good stuff, isn't it, queen?
Echinacea,   turmeric,   augmentation.
My mother making tea: she knows
I can't sleep, and skylarks. Moving with the shame,
and skylarks.

Yourself, a Stranger

Those who could hear me were perplexed.   I saw
I see I am   dancing bitterness.

Bitter nitrogen;
campaign ads
answers to rhetorical questions
Banksy-style Molotov cocktails
            filled with flowers -
I love the taste of bitterness.
Don't offer me a peach.
I want to be on Sir's consolatory Twitter show,
offer back a sodden mouth.
Sounds cannibalistic. I'm not not into it.

Something
something abomination.   Something
something sinister in the air
of small towns ringed by fields grown brown
with thoughtless use.   Someone someone
flying overhead. Wheeling and wheeling. Make me
a mouse in your claw.   Make me
a hand grenade between legs.   The revolution
answers rhetorical questions, the questions
at dinner tables
shoved into the mouths of children choked -

congressmen and priests and CEOs ask:
Why can't I feel below the neck?
What if there is no life of the spirit?
Do you want these people in your neighborhood?

I can't feel below the neck because I
beat my arms against closed locker doors, my fists
into my face.   If there is no life of the spirit
then you have been right all along
                                        if then
there are no bodies saints growing tomatoes in their gardens,
no tiger lilies, snapdragon; no wild
bodies hyacinths, then

this is the answer and the carnival; you carry
in advance the ending of the night,
congratulatory confetti,
solo cups, forlorn panties, masks forgotten there —
I have some to spare —
then you and I will tire of the schemes between my thighs -
there, breathe out, find Bibles on the nightstands,
unused, fluffy handcuffs tucked in dresser drawers.

Ask your most frustrating uncle if he feels
the land beneath his feet, the woman in his heels;

ask, from minimum safe distance, with spray paint
or with riot shield   the police, if they
have looked forward to killing
themselves, after all this.   Ask the CEOs and priests.
O and your fascist father.

I bitternessed
the dance and talked it out.   We've solved everything,
or I was another in a long line
of solvents.   I carry a bitterness with me -
a greening shard, good enough to eat.

Further Excavations

I am, like the version of me in October
splitting the difference between two names,
ready under a pine tree in the local Recreational Nature Area.
There I, child in the riverbed and on the needles
soft and riveting, am at my limit.

I in retrospect never said *I can only see*
bathwater blue up to my eyes, leaking
from inside.   These factory seams, I aim to please.

You've heard me say once if a hundred times   my first
      time trying *this,*
waiting tables, catching the strap, writing about sex without
pretending to be Pablo Neruda,   pretending to be a boy
pretending to be a wolf   pretending to be a king.

With my eyes you can see
the ground softened for my burial.   Now bury me at sea,
a sea of brown pine needles under an October sky.

But. Instead of suicide.

This numb, extraordinary mouth.
Absurd chasing of the next —
which will not satisfy.

This year (under close inspection) turns out the
same suggestions
as the ones before. More. Natalie Diaz
for president. Then end the presidents for good.
Kiss my ass.

Listen.
Listen. I have told myself *not yet*
because death may be overrun
with crocodiles. Here I am kept.
Haven't I kept enough from you?
Telling you I am is not enough. Let me try again. I am:

Be Cruel.[1]

In our years of study on the test subject, we found that she does not register
much feeling below the neck. Small burns from baking sheets,
subzero gusts of wind, a hand between her legs. We observed, in fact,
that for her, masturbation is as automatiç as a lunch-hour meal.
Experienced in the mechanics of orgasm she has not dared
explore Antarctica. Perhaps in fifty years when the ice thaws
she will submerge herself in a salted sea
and Coriolis, from the bottom of her feet through her fingertips,
a conduit for larger force.
Or rise into space, orienting herself so that she,
like all galaxies, starts to rush away from ours
into a shifting red.
Until such a time she has methods — begs blows, opens her coat to the cold.
They are partial measures. Stopgaps.
Once I get my body right, she writes.
She lies awake in bed, most nights,
fantasizing about anesthetic and bloody scalpels
pressed against her skin. We're going to turn her inside out,
and why stop there? Take the interior mind and expose it: give those nerve
endings something to work against, flush of air,
alarm of constant touch. Pin her wrists to the bed, draw blood,
drown her in the bathtub. Turn her violence outward from the years'
internal crush, too, let her lash out —

— snap ligament from bone, body from wing —
and when they form again, healed and blurred by scar,
be unrecognizable.   We hypothesize that only then
will she allow herself to feel bioelectric human hands.
We observe that it begins in the brain, a delicate
thread pulled tight, then tighter.   Beginning with one unspun.

Tied to the bed she begs, *please devour my mind.*
Please. My mind will not let me go.   *Please release me.*
Make good use of me, before I lose myself completely.
Unsheathe scalpel over her. Taste green ruin in the air.

---

1 Researcher X. A., against the wishes of his superiors, includes his own work on the following page; a poem written in response to two years of study of the subject and a series of unrecorded, personal conversations between X and the subject. This poem, *Be Cruel.*, was given along with the rest of the study documentation to our patrons at the end of ████████, leading to some confusion at the financial report and outline of the study's results included therein, and subsequently to the firing of X from the Institute.

A Toast to Piss

A bad girl wants to finish writing so she can play. A bad girl doesn't pause before the keystroke, feels herself up, with a need to finish before going out. Look, her eye. Glint sinister. Ninety-eight dollar bodysuit. Don't bother breaking out the good wine. What's good is what gets you there. She doesn't drink wine. She asks, is this happiness? Makes lists. Kiss her. A bad girl asks. A bad girl begs. How would you know this is mercy? Mercy on the national top shortage and the will to rebellion. Mercy on the heartstoppers and queerbaiters. Love can, like anything. Love, unlike your piss. A bad girl wants to become a biblically accurate angel -eyes and holes and eyes, justice unbound by law. Slut. S-l-u-t slut. Porn is cheating a boner is a Johnson don't remind her she's a bottom — unless you're her ex standing over her with a knack for knots the right amount of taut. Porn is cheating it made you soy it mated with a hotwife it is stuck can't you help it. Sex should be between a dyke and her boyfriend. Sacrosanct and artful authenticity. Know thy body, stiff unmoved. A bad girl doesn't want you to flake. A bad girls sobs because she's so high.

Won't somebody piss in her mouth? She's after all been so good, so rigid, against all odds pious to the point of privation. Morning fast. Generosity to angels. A rebellion inherited. Not I. Not incandescent. Not devout. Least of all. Stealing glances. Envy or. A bad girl tops. A bad girl fucks you in your office. A bad girl's fingers would, forever if they could. Clips her fingernails. Notice to vacate. To clip her wings. Doesn't even fantasize. Love, like your piss. A bad girl makes dinner in her bodysuit. A bad girl pulls the flood. A bad girl likes your pain as much as. Whimper. Ask again. Say it again. A bad girl raises her glass. Room given to hush. A smile parts her lips.

Disclosure

I am evidence.
Dredged fear's blue bruised
rotting   (whalefall below
                           calm harbor) –
until my berry of a head
is crushed.
Come join me
to you. Add me to the list of possibilities, semicolon, fuckable,
asterisk –
what good God –
fearing laminate loves only
genitalia?
Do your prefer pussy swollen by beestings or by desire,
uneven labia wave sculpted flesh asymmetrical
and dark?
What is in the emptiness you cannot
fit yourself inside?

Here's an idea, investors of America:
a clothing brand for everyone who needs
a shield   who refuses to be disguised.
Dying on a day that isn't today;
enjoying all her yellow, dizzy flowers.

Give us pockets:

for needles or three-month-pill refills
delivering us to us
dangerous, intoxicating.

Pockets are parachutes.
Pockets for aspiring gunslingers.
Pockets to slip you pills, prestige, esoterica - let these pockets
be the red curtain of intermission before the final act,
a musical number which brings together
all of us, living and dead, to recount
what we've learned.   Pockets into which the poems
the names of our lost siblings
can compress or fold into the shape of swans.
And a pocket for the Lady Chablis,
Grand Empress of Savannah.
Give us pockets that remain empty in anticipation
of that longing, which comes to us on New Year's.

Forty-five million
eight hundred thousand nine-hundred twenty-nine
people have something important to tell you (give or take).
Leave us haloed with pain,
Wilson-brother broken noses,
pray for us with both hands
clasped around our neck asking
why we do not give way like green birches to the axe.

Here is our trick:

what trans is.   You already know.

It lives in you like birdsong unheard

as you attend to your own image in the grass,

Christ's face on white Wonderbread,

but not my mother's in mine.

As vine threads between fences and in years

pulls the whole thing down.   We became drills that
    hesitate against

the permafrost of our bodies, remain

narrow shining, arriving in our power.

What midnight twirls and nightswims gave us the breath

of water: when nowhere in air

wanted us, we became ballerinas of our drowning.

Congregation

— there are no trans girls to come to my funeral.
No enby hotties in crop tops to explain my rage in eulogy and
afterwards describe
the miserable glory of my kinks; no butch trans women
to come to my readings and tell me I don't have to do it alone,
my delusions of grandeur can evaporate like summer puddles &
the tadpoles in them will be saved, all saved; no high-school
trans girls
to whom I taught *The Bell Jar* to tell me
dying isn't a wake-up call,
none in a hotel with lousy carpet to let you know
your life before was just some bad dream brought on by
indigestion,
there was no name imposed, there was no body hair
or laser hair removal, no impossible bra,
no confusion whether wanting to be a mother made you -
Let the trans girls
go home from my funeral and decide on that night
to pool together whatever they have left after copays
clothes surgery and drought
to buy the very first trans bar in a better world;
let the sober trans girls buy an old arcade machine, put in
the back,
let them fall over one another
laughing at how bad they are at billiards and

about being so incredible at chess,
let them remain invulnerable outside the bar wishing they
 could smoke cigarettes
and smoking weed instead. I want to be at this funeral so badly
 I have to live:

a broken cup glued together,
the lining of gold common to all things remade.
Raise a toast for all the funerals carried out in secret, as loud as
 we can,
on the street corners, too late for anyone to hear.

Section I. Field Notes [From Sections I-XI of the Final Report]

Our first two years of study on the subject were, if we may be permitted a moment of emotion before diving into carefully considered study and the facts therein, exhausting. It stretched several of our leading researchers to their breaking points. Being constantly on alert for signs of weakness or moments of particularly intense delusions; spending so much time not only watching its reactions, tears, laughter, boredom, and so on in real time, but studying those emotions, the microexpressions of the body and face, afterwards, incorporating the intensity of subjective experience into a narrative of objective data.

Seven months into the subject's experimental and dangerous artificial hormone regimen, we exposed it to the most difficult test of its commitment to its delusion to that point in the study. We provided a not insubstantial sum to its father in order to stimulate a test of emotional durability: the father, ███, made contact to insinuate that the mother of the subject, ███, was responsible for its delusions. It should be noted that this was our working hypothesis until our interview with the subject's mother on ███, when the information acquired closed that avenue of research and opened several others.

The subject, according to our interviews (eight total between ███ ███, the period of greatest emotional intensity according to our regular MRI tests done on the subject over the course of the study), considered detransition several times over the course of this period after the initial contact with its father. In fact, this moment of instability led to several months of extended dissociation. We would mark this approach as one to continue investigating with vigor and a keen observing eye.

Dr. ███ was removed from the course of the project, was the first to point out that the subject often seemed to be watching us back, despite our instructions to act as if we were not there. Even months after this initial suggestion of a mutuality in our observation,

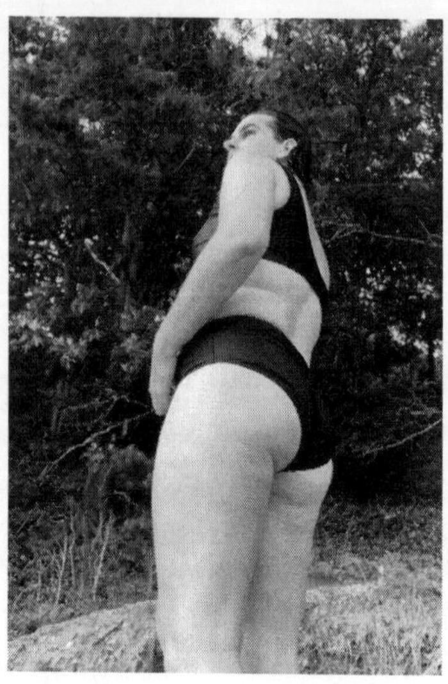

it remains both impossible to prove and impossible to ignore. It has become obsessed with the threat of physical violence, despite its unlikeliness; we observe, saying nothing, the creep of legislation passed to eliminate the transgender from public life. Even as we are pleased to see the success of our patronss in their other avenues of work against the transgender delusion, it makes the more skittish among us nervous that our work will no longer be necessary.

All that aside, we learned a great deal about the subject. It is easily influenced for others, both to the benefit and the detriment of the delusion which consumes it. We are perpetually surprised by how many others are willing to participate in its delusion. It is akin to a bird struggling its way into flight.

ARDOR

Layaway

after Galina Rymbu

Lie down on the floor of your bathroom,
if you can.   Remember the last time you were too sick
to go to school — I'll remember the same thing
at the same time — how I, half-joking, eulogized myself
when I had the flu.
Remember how alien the tiles were against us.
The uncomfortably cold, smooth surface —
like the war stories of our grandfathers, lacking names,
details, context — polished stones — or better yet,
beachglass shorn enough of edges to take home
and put in a jar —   what is friendly,
when well, becomes unbearable in sickness.
Blankets, bed itself, heat, our softnesses.

Now that we're together,
I'll ask you, though
you haven't earned this poem yet.

How much does bottom surgery cost, does insurance cover it,
should I put my pussy on layaway?
What if I can only afford an econi-pussy,
no cupholders, leather interior, or rims?
The Spirit airlines of pussies, a K-Mart pussy, a lemon of
    a pussy
that can't be trusted for long trips —
Zipper, Velcro for convenience?

I had the audacity to think deflection
could buy me some relief. But the hospital needs cold hard
    cash,
iron and diamonds dug from mountains, paid in clotted blood
and blackened lung - the doctors need me to represent the
    community,
to write a dozen letters' confirmation
I am devout in my delusions   (here I am, zealous
    in my doubt).

The insurance company will take oil and gold.
To save money, my new pussy can be more abstract —
I'll find a surgeon outside the mainstream, on the cheap,
to make a Monet pussy which only looks good from the middle
    distance
or a Dali pussy   microwaved too long.

Better not to bother; better start fundraising,
write a children's book written in careful metaphor about my
pussy to get clicks
and controversy, end up on the cover of the *New York Post,*
my pussy leaked online, my pussy reviewed on YouTube,
my pussy ranked against other pussies by *Buzzfeed,*
my pussy winning prizes, my pussy   against the
    tile of the bathroom floor.

I admit, I'm dizzy about surgery.
Consults, forms, cleanses, recoveries; bloody, boring, long and dull —
asking if it's what I want, if it's really worth it.
Funny how your brain keeps things from you.
We're here because I hated my body as a teenager,
kept the feeling in a pit in a snowy plain.
Fear that no one would touch me, want me   I spirited away on a warm wind
over New York in August,
thick with the odors of trash, human sweat, and exhaust.
This need, I kept here on the bathroom floor,
ignoring it as best I could.

This is where I lay when I realized that this was not the only world,
that someone moved on the other side.   Where I knew
that my will could shape my breasts, that in me lay
well, *this* —
which has as many arms
and lives in as deep a darkness as the giant squid,
blind and milky, beside my eely fears and reptilian anxieties.
We're here in case I forget how to piss, or never learn again,
get purpling infection, a plum split by ripeness.
Those fears are with us on the bathroom floor,

the floor of the operating theater.
This poem will exist before and after,
long after the fears have stopped their desperate,
breathy flopping on the cold tile,
after the anxieties skitter away through crevices
to their own little world of plumbing and mayflies.

It doesn't matter anyway if I can piss
but whether I can explain it to the curious,
the passersby who come intrigued to the floor of the bathroom
and ask if I am a boy or a girl
if I am here to intrude on women's spaces
if I am here to win at college sports,
if I regret my mutilation. If I know that God despises me.
Come see for yourself.
After a few months of our little rest,
pussy fully integrated into society,
the floor of the bathroom
sprouts. Ivy first and creepers, thin weeds between
grout, and out of me, too, come Kazakh tulips, calla lily and
        violets —
out of the brutal words and the holes they tore in me —
vaginoplasty   clitoroplasty   labiaplasty
like bulldozers   TNT   scalpels.
The clear evidence of blows should be enough

for you to gather conclusions among the wild onions.
So come ask me your questions.
I didn't bring you here to watch me assemble into greenery
or listen to my bad jokes — it is lonely here
in the way I imagine places without life at all are lonely —
a bathroom floor, the surface of Mars,   our Moon's ridges.

There's no hope   here, or anywhere   of curing this fever
like a cloud of bees.   I am also the bees.
The willow, too, especially her weeping.
I want a pussy, a century or a minute in,
buried so deeply under moss
the rush of clear water coming, from deep in me —
so you can't hear me at all.   And you won't
until I want you to, when your hands are on me
        ready to receive, be received in turn —
when you can't see me, nor I, any longer, see you.

Extinguisher

I am,   breathlessly
either   or. Last holdout
of the classic composers: she writes musically,
in flux,   nicknamed the "Raindrop,"
by George Sand. An etude on being neither nor.
An Elise to be for.

Pray for yourself.   Paths you haven't tread,
tread in secret.
Look in my mouth:
I have a woman's taste
in sorrow.
Not only that. *She couldn't sing*
she was too old to remember lyrics,
but she could still play
a submerged piano,
fond, delayed.

Call the accumulation
of secrets salvation and the boot upon the neck
salvation,   breaking of a mare
salvation.   Pristine, vanilla,
happy, comfortable,   goldfinch
cracked by glass.   Thucydides
had seven ships   a world to lose. And I

a broken spear.   Years of loneliness
didn't end with estrogen;
the rainstorm at your door refuses offering.

Homegrown

This isn't the first time I've gone to sleep
with period blood dried on my inner thigh.
TMI? Sorry, we're way past that, chief.
Ask how deep the trenches go.
Ask the angler's light.

I am an animal of festival, wrath,
exhibition,   wit, and fingering.
The trenching floor
is crushed and cold. Where I belong.

Leave me your womb.

Please.
Where are the children?

Please.
Hold this poem like your own.
There is too much to explain
to you, clean up and serve
on a plate.
Taste anyway. Sunflower
seed, American Spirit, absinthe, April mud.

I throw the windows open,
am torn astray by crows.

Last time I knew what I was
I was wrong.
Leave me as in all things,
unfinished;   that is to say, perfected.

Yarrow

You fill me up contrary.
Gasp and ask to break
the surface tension in your cup — I do —
and you   at least, you
color me, don't mind dye spreading
in water. Its cephalopod curl.
Take care of me,
be sure to hurt:
I concede to brands & breakage.
Rip my pages and spit me aloud.
Make me something that is.
That rhymes.   That lives in ringing throat.

Dragonfly

My hands are preoccupied. Pierced
by sewing needle; electrons, in entangled pairs,
spin when the other spins.
I'm in debt to you; mistook red for blue and blue for red
in you.

Sex in poetry, at its best, relies on household objects,
fruit, meat.
I am cold and honeycrisp
after your bite; open, gouged and frayed.
A blue crab among the reeds.

Bathwater leaking across the floor;
a collapsed glacier's thrust into the sea below.
What's worse than wounded?
Compromised. As in given more
than I wanted,   less than I might.
Risked reaching out for what I am most afraid to touch.

Service Review

Am I still intact? — let's say not, and draw
a boundary through a still-omnipresent country
to unmake me; let's say I fail again to make myself apparent
and pieces started coming loose — so idle
I curdle, milk speckled in husk
wherever it's tugged off.
Fingernails candied at the root. Did you intend to leave me
with these inseams from nipple to sternum
up my jaw in preparation for a shattering.
Is this a consequence?
                                        Am I grown?
Will fruiting bodies come to me in the night and fall by
    morning,
in ripeness promised running brown and delicacy spread
of wetness deeper than the fruit's, the *thump* and silence of
    the fall?
I wanted enough to roll a string of thunder off my shoulders
and douse us all in rain. The lightning throws fits,
storm's clean sweep to wipe us acidic as a riddled lime.

Ode to the Surgical Site

I've been a good little dummy for doctors
to practice on,   so limp & so willing, gone
briskly into the lidocaine snowstorm,
indebted to their array
of vacuums, lasers, shock and twitch –
give me shape
let me ape the better,
bitter women of that century.
Do you recognize me? Will this self,
looking out, spreading her legs
for the strap stripping me of signifier, inverting
the standards of society, her norms
in recovery - will she
recognize herself?   A temptation:
to erase it all, to wash me out starlet blonde,
gone Marilyn Monroe.   Powder
the incisions, divisions of current
from former self, and chalk up that distant future
to a down payment on me, improved.   Renewed.
Rejuvenated   gassed.
Unclockable, time passes.
She, unbidden,
looks back in disdain.

What is this unformed thing, this glimmer
in the frost?   *Why do I remember what it was like*
to be so unfounded in my faith in womanhood?
I cannot tell you either.   I cannot
write of my face, the face my god made —
a god in a white coat
having been invited in —
invited, a bat, to rapture me with wing.

Innocents

for Alexander Cheves

I am a rose-city-self today. Motherly, shame comfortable,
    & quiet,
amidst intestines   A rosewater douche,
inherited perfume.   At the airport
I trailed half a dozen Mormon men returning from their
    missions.
In the women's bathroom I cradled the head of Elder Josiah
    Wood
to my breast, fawn eyes, dammed yearning.
I made milk from prayer.
Are you an angel?   Today
and at all tomorrow's parties, Josiah.
A braless angel, armpit hair.
It means stillness over Mt. Hood –
a splash of cloud, a leaping Arctic fox;
it means feeding you if nothing else my flesh, digging
a knife into my forearm between ulna and radius
so you may, there, sip.
Is there such a place as heaven?
There is, Josiah, but heaven isn't for you.
Heaven is for her prodigal children
who never return home, who spend their lives straying,
straying a vocation.
Home is for the fisted, the knockers on after-midnight doors
literal, assholes,
home is for the transformed, the touched,

dedicated, riotous, colorful, cleansed
by salt water, which we (truehearted) know will not make us
    innocent.
Longing deep inside their used mouths
after their backshots
to rest awhile alongside their fellows,
the failed soldiers in our hearts   and hearths and hallways,
stealing our leftovers, stumbling in at three in the morning.
There is no weariness from hiding
nor from telling everyone you meet.
Innocents have nothing to hide, nor decide, Josiah.
Heaven is the heavy table where we gather for a meal that lasts
forever.   There is wine
comfortable furniture to lie, touching one another
in heaven; there are no condoms there,
no memory of pain to make us hesitate in love.
I will spend eternity
tongue deep —
there is nothing like my devotion, even in heaven.
You are dear in ways your world has told you, you are not.
I was a goddess of the rot. Lost all grace.
The desirous eye, rum & dance on moonlit beaches,
stumbling through sand. Until you allow it in, my son,
remain empty.   No rosy self.
No sluttery.   No heaven.

A Swim in a Pond in the Rain / Sonnet 116

I had no body of my own,
the fire of drought country after a single match,
the riot of August wildflowers hardy enough to live til fall's first
frost.
Of course I'm afraid of you.
The way your collarbone is pressed to the thin fabric of your shirt —
of course I'm afraid.

I keep a lantern burning.

Ballroom Dancing

The sky rides hubcap colors; she
a Roman chariot with a ballroomy twist
a glitz   peregrination   a desire.
I decant phrases both
needed and not:
thirty pages of verse.
            trimmed spinifex,
Bliss.
The sky knights
you verminous,
preachy, keen.
That chariot –
a Bucharest she knows,
a Pittsburgh, a Juliet
and dormouse Romeo
squeaking under her boots.
You pinch crimped my thumb
until my mind bled for it, beneath
a table. Eagerly the hush.
I between a *self* and box
marked *other*.
Wax seal, list of baby names,
their meanings, an incitation
to run. She would not know
the chrome, the sky's feckless heart

at home. I give her two
decayed wings and say:
thirty pages of verse.
cut august,
Kiss.
If you knew you would know
what ligaments
heckle me beneath this
gown.
You would see that while I appear
an embossed star, I am held
together all by my dark domain,
not to be seen, but witnessed.

Authentic Derangement

What this town needs is prescribed fire, an ecological
scene-setting, scouring rats, cats, roaches, the obligatory
coyote running before stampede ephemera.
Carry the moss that shades your eyes and monuments.
A cicada husk, southern dusk, walkability
for the rest. Wherever you're going is a
haphazard blocks away, in a city's
unsavory history, its guileless present.
Ladies, whether by design or the school of design,
your blouses fall apart
seamlessly, your tattoos take trending to mean
artful, your piercings prick your plumage.
Your song too,
lacks devotion. Greedily
I slurp miserable mothers. Greedily
in the dark with fathers. Screaming at the barista
for mishearing you. Screaming at your daughter
for mishearing you. As burning
accelerates in the company of every lousy commuter
and the single vivid fantasy of suicide, I cannot write poetry.
Only so long left for leering in the park.
Only so many coyotes left to hound towards
another mirrored city likewise hounding
drifters, animal and otherwise, towards an ocean
that is a glue trap. Ladies, I cannot tell you

whether you will be found guilty
or whether guilt will pursue you
as a lynx pursues a hare. And whether being torn open
will be the same as blossoming I cannot say.
But there are infinite outcomes
to a crisis of faith, and only one of them is return.

Night Reception

for A.

Christ, but she reminds me.
Am I vertiginous? TSA don't check the face.
I didn't shave last night, and by my own word
am all *they* today. Girl, don't even say it, Lord knows
I know what I did. Much love for the Man-Ray
and its devotees. Girl drink with me.
Twenty-one hours straight.
Candle coming up with new ends to burn from,
an ex-husband doctoring atoms.
Carry your club outfit with you
at all times, for emergencies. You never know
when you will have a lumpectomy at thirty-six
and go out to drink for a friend, gone.

You have a great energy, someone says to me, which translated
    means
you're a Cambridge 6, but I like your hair.

Circle you round. Pursue and retreat.
Apologize sweet. You didn't need.
Kissed outside the 7-11 sounds better than kissed adjacent to
    the 7-11
so we kissed outside the 7-11. Time has it in mind
to let me know I have seen so little. Few hospital beds and
    courtrooms,

none of them mine, no divorce papers, health scares.
New Order T-Shirt. Brainy girls from peasants. The terrorist
state.
Coming to the hotel room like Romeo.
Sit with contentment: no longer writhing, a worm on a rained-
out sidewalk.
Content with my fourth shot, content with four hours' sleep.
The underside of the world. Hahvahd Yahd. I do have great
hair.
Girl! Drink with me!
I consider what remains. The common air, the tears, your lips.
Promise. I promised the Gulf of Finland long ago,
the shallow water sunk with submarines and heavy metals,
I promised guests to get them home safely, and I did.
I always do.

Even the exiled. Meow meow. All my kitties are bad and
all my kitties are lost, like me. Run a hand through fur.
99 luftballoons. Hand on collarbone damp with sweat. Sting,
strut.
Leap into faith that didn't doubt, didn't stray -
Christ but I am reminded of so much, yet.

Twenty-Five Stems

for T.C.

For the sake of regimen,
of essential, unimportant tasks —
we've run low on yogurt, fruit,
the sink drain needs cleaning out —
for the sake of all that I must pretend
there is no such thing as a woman.
Not, certainly, one specific person
who fragmented my head
all manners of glass, of petals.
A windshield shattered marigolds.
And your eyes: if the heat of melted
steel, on cooling,
cooled into oils, resolved into canvases.
You remember: the Pushkin
State Museum of Fine Arts. The portrait
of that hunched, gambling genius.
You must remember. You've lived
in my mind. I could never chase you out.

If on darker nights
on darker plains
in some lightless sanctuary
the moonlight made a river flow
between us and the stars,
it would not be so cold

as to take my breath
more than you have taken my breath,
run off with it like a child,
holding it out of my reach.
In a world where I can breathe you in,
what need, then, of atmosphere?

If I could give you one gift
it would be a lock of hair
for you to curl around your fingers
and pull, to beckon me
wherever I am.
If I could give you ten gifts
they would be all these estranged fingers
allegedly my own, that you made yours.
That I made mine.
I gave you all these gifts.
And received –

I lived this long and didn't know
the potential
woven into my skin like tapestries;
how has it never occurred to me
as it did last night, and this morning,
and now, again, that I have breasts?

And you have not touched them, yet.
The great masters
go up in flames:
in that smoke written
delirious my love your name.

In Absentia

None of them
have children.
I whisper –
you should take me back to my hotel.
My pockets are empty,
and my blood is full.
Mothers scold,
daughters stay out late.
I've been tried, found guilty
in absentia. And what a hellcat.
Make me strange.
Diseased. Distressed, in need of urgent care,
correction, the love of a good woman –
her punishment –
bite the iron cage's bars, her punishment
a lash on the thigh and bottoms of her feet.
Her delicious, leaves her
fierce lonely, uncuttable,
dark as Trondheim
bright as police flashlight.
Still as Spanish moss in the air before a hurricane,
I have not come to my strength.
Give me guilty over pristine.
I leave a fiery swath behind me
from Atlanta to the bluegold sea.

Section II. Field Notes [From Subsection XIXA: Sexual and Romantic Relationships of the Transgender]

IMAGE 2G ID: A biological human male lays across a bed, partially buried under white blankets. Its head and upper back are visible. The subject looks directly at the camera or the photographer with its one visible eye.

This image was taken in the first year of our three-year study of the subject (20XX–20XX). Immediately after it changed its name in public usage from ████████ to ████████, it entered into a polyamorous relationship with a biological woman. This photograph was taken by one of the subject's extra-relational partners, a sex worker and dancer.

On a scale of 0–10, 0 being feminine and 10 being masculine, 902 male participants rated the subject an average of 8.2 points — more masculine than several nontransgender subjects presented as alternatives to the subject. In this instance it is obvious that the delusion of womanhood is co-created between the photographer and the subject. A picture of itself, at this point eight months into the process of artificial hormone treatment, could not do alone what a picture taken by another can accomplish.

The same can be said of the subject's sexuality. Our team of researchers assigned to the study of the subject's sexuality have been hard at work understanding the link between sexual trauma, C-PTSD, ASD, and gender identity disorder, making important progress in linking together mental disorders and illnesses in the creation of the transgender delusion. And the key to all of this is the enabling of a transgender subject by its partners: a belief, against biology and reason, that this *is* a woman.

MILK

A Solitary Feast

for S

Two weeks later, and I've gone backwards, from acceptance
to rage — I was disposed of,
the way one disposes of six-dollar panties
a year after buying — still holding together
while the roses and lace, faded, paling, and frayed,
lose their glamor.   But darling,
we agreed all relationships, connections,
all bristlecone pines and tectonic shifts, come
to their own conclusions.
There's vanity in longing —
clinging with my papery fingertips
to the frosted surface of our Moon,
trying to pin the tides with a box of thumbtacks,
looking at the memory of you like I didn't.
Now I must, cannot, reconcile a grieving world.
One where grief meets expectation.

Death by a thousand romantic journal entries,
photos in portrait mode from the cold pandemic months
we could not see one another   except on swingsets
by desolate elementary schools,   Lutheran churches
under the spare branches of a maple older than our city.
Reconciliation, darling.   Lithographs.
Temperance.   You asked, *has anyone looked at you*
as if they love you?

Has anyone looked at you as if they would hold you, then let
you go? I.

What else could we dispose of — shuttered winter,
snow going begging on a darkened street,
dissolving like sugar on hot asphalt?
Our first times. I became another person then,
someone who, for lack of better word,
was good — see dictionary for definition:
good, (adj.), looking up from your notebook and hearing trumpets,
tucking a napkin into your collar, tea with honey and ginger,
the person who is content missing the last bus.

Someone, I promise, in another time
will remember us — will remember you and I
on the path back home, along the river,
before dawn on a May morning.
The fragments
and flowers that remain, beside the helmets and the chariots,
a single broken spear, a lily plucked and then brought
to the fringe of rotting in the vase.
A red comet overhead. A disallowed kiss
when I came home from New York last winter —
you had missed the gush & gnaw & wound of my mouth
so much you would have written me into existence

if I hadn't been there — I felt that, I knew it then.
There is, I'm sure, or want to be sure,
beauty in what wilts despite the watering,
loveliness obscure under reminders
of the end -the ominous loveliness of lightning
reflected on unsettled water, a concert under rain. If nothing else lasts,
hurt and love remain entwined.   This is how it was meant to be.

Alstroemeria (Thine)

I've been a week uneasy.
Floating around the living room, a slipping husband's bourbon.
Parts of me go missing, alstroemeria,
petals dipped in blood, fragments of onion skin, no hands,
springform pans, ice rings near the door. No eyes.

I shouldn't, but I believe in dreams.
Not always what they say —   the ripples, rather, of
         dark water
outward from the threshold's cross.
So and now the alstroemeria, blood of thine,
my rosy sheets — I roughing weep.
I wake up sore   congested, discontent.
Oh jealousy, green as snowbells' stems in March
I find you salted, as all feeling, in my mouth,
where I have swallowed
glasswort, half sea half mud half sour.

And it was mine too.   I had no eyes.
                 When you cried
in my arms: beheaded. Don't look now;
my alstroemeria, I can't live this way.
Petals dipped in lung. Fresh water, every morning.

[ ]

Having a different story for each set of eyes is no mean feat.
Eye, allure   eye enrage
devour eyes on vines choking
back.   One backhoe tearing trees,
fire's scour, and begins.   Smoke
in the throat, a swarm of wasp trickling
thick, liquid almost smooth.   Hello again.
It begins & ends in a geologic age.
A brash proof: nature's will
hustles to rid us of us. Good
riddance.   The choke begins & ends in Temple Bar
after a show, epilogued by another police
report. He / she / they said the title of the book.
She / he / it disgraces limits.
Saved from senselessness by it, the kudzu
and their burning, lichens on the north wall, killing
makes us whole as living. In another breed of quiet.
                                One variable
amid your constancy, devotion. I love you, X. Punish me,
X.   X *equals choke.* Where
X is between, without; lived and will live; bitter & bright.

Wheel of Fortune

Wherever water carries themself to
a body, whether by ascending aorta
or by descent into a tunnel
dressed in THANK YOU
shopping bags, in blessed once-used
needles, in condoms and in greening
vile foam, wherever they carry
my cellulite like a tectonic plate
bubbling into islands
and my leg hair deforested and returning
for the sake of a beauty only my eyes believe in,
wherever it is swept up inside me
at the ocean that I so fear
because she is my mother and I crawled
from her and learned that air
would kill me while she held me,
and that that was all I wanted.
Am I orgasmic?
Am I your girl?
Can I after ages which have seen
most species of living things
disappear from the world
without even a bone
in the fossil record
forget that first learned breath?

Wherever water carries me
you carry me, wherever
I am infiltrated and infiltrate in turn
the body of a night heron
or all the night herons
along the river,
yellowing, prehistoric eyes,
bodies blossoming toxins
bodies blossoms seas,
bodies blossoming the river
into you and into me
the lift to fall to falling
into me, into you.

Colossus Redux

after Sylvia Plath

I am your enemy,   another
in a line of gawkers come worshipping
(as if to Lenin's tomb)
by your memory, hushed — do not speak,
as the wrists of this woman, they say,
will shatter —   a champagne flute, enduring aria.
Every young woman wants to be you,
I want to be every young woman.
        Are we enemies
when we have an enemy in common;
gynecologists masquerading as fathers masquerading
as minor fascists,   private
obedience: whitewashed skulls,
seagull songs,   drills' shriek?
And would not your memorial flame
serve better as a chandelier, a centerpiece,
a prize —
no reward better than skinny beauty
gaining, we promise, a little weight
in the hospital.
Yeats' oven,
I need ask, must we be enemies
too?   I can spray you down and rub the rust
away, spread it in the stead of ashes, if you explain -
what did she taste of?   Red comet,

lady Lazarus, what didn't you
devour?   And a plate
of bread and butter. A scattering of bows.
Faith sown in fields outside;
a colossus centuries in reaping.

Trans Girl Gangbang at the End of the World

Lights out on the West Coast,
sirens calling out to trash heaps.
The microplastics in me now
are the silicone cocks of futurity.   The hunger,
unrecognizable (disguised as tension,
fear, as weariness), meets lust in the middle and gets
wires crossed. Like myth.
Let the reader parse which is which.
Rather than quoting conversations
only you and I were privy to,
let's usher in our guests to this
fluorescent-scalded office.   And
once, maybe, in those fragile moments where
I am the slow shift of glass in cathedral windows
downward, thickening at one end of centuries, I'll thrive.
Fold their names under my tongue
like cherry lozenges, so suture-sweet,
and stop praying. Skin as smooth as a whale-eye stone,
intermingled hands careless of age & tender
like the light as it plays with dust in the Hagia Sophia.

Translucence

A whole city in bad disguise, black-coated failing
to pass themselves as crows.   I am red-feathered,
preen interruption. Gossiping to myself
about the stares of Midwestern mothers passing by:
a simple, dizzy thing, preoccupied
entirely, tasting sooted air
with the crushed waver of heat eluding grates
spilling, like the eyes & javelins of rebelling angels,
up, and only upward.   I break when
unwitnessed — witnessing keeps me aloft,
floating from gaze to gaze, a starlet from another decade
unconcerned, and broken — an exotic animal,
gusto, bravado, spilling crumbs, elegant, disgusting.

Most of all, the brilliance in me —
the way I hoped to glitz, to crisp
as water did in that long ago ice-storm,
hanging the weight of full-grown-men and their obsessions
from the telephone lines, ash, elm, oak, pine,
temporary as the drip   wetclear melting falling
then refreezing.   On the grounds
of insanity, give me lenience.
I lived machinishly, possessed by
a witch in those mousefursilver years.

Find me now translucent,
frosted glass, in the cinema watching I-don't-know-what.
One might say that nothing ends. That this exhausted
    lighthouse, cycles
moon, shore, moon, ships, rocks, shore —
that this unsleeping stare.   Is fixed on you.
Come. Come bear my eyes.
Unload this accumulated weight, let loose
these long-untethered isles held only by my will.

Green Over Grey

for Juniper

We are all Atlas. Bad backs, hunched over desks
hitting CTRL + Z every eleven minutes like the good drones
we are, making soap on Etsy & on the side studying social
work — not
too late. That's the world that won't end.
Oh clamor. Green over grey at the end of May.

Green over grey. Am I abdicating the responsibility of living
things
by making French toast at night, roasting potatoes in the oven?
Watching the worst *Star Wars* for the comedy.
Don't say hate-watching after the Roe v. Wade leak is wrong.
Don't say that the way we found ourselves coming back to
our bodies
after so long away was wrong, because it was an oil painting
life,
we lived delicious, brown-sugar in oatmeal hours, it was
green over grey in the beginning of May, smoke from nearby
fires
perfuming up our hair.
Dog bless, it's ours.   Dog bless,
possession needs not prey upon the weak. O how strong
submission. How soaked our blanket.   Don't say gay,
say Sapphic, say that some love ships and spears
and bloody beaches best.

We are all Achilles, know we would rather
broken backs for our own sake
than to be kings of all the breathless dead.   Feet in the
        grass,
rain on the face, green among grey. The cliffs in southern
        Illinois &
how quiet the Ohio ran, except the calling of some stray geese.

And your eyes green over grey, these days that sow blooming.
Consider so spectacular a summer,
fainting from the heat. The body. Your body.
Needs. Wants. Hand held fast to bed by hand, and under sea.
        The smell of salt cooled
        by a slow breeze from far away.

Grey into green, this early May evening after work,
counting up the baked goods left after Friday's rushed leisure.
Green into grey, dropping wings at table thirty-two -
put a finger down if you grieve people who are better for being
        without you,
and you without them. Put a finger
inside me if grief feels like fear feels like a sinus headache
feels like greens gone bad feels
lucid with desire, deep drunken, sorry and stateless.

And imagine your poems go on and on, that *you* go on and on?
How I remember changes as much as what.
I remember rushing from event to event past
each little thing, waiting to be burned, but there was no
    burning.

Handfasted, no fear.
She plants our eyes in seedbeds so that all we've seen
will grow into more than we were.
No fear.   We are all
Sappho and our work is wintered in the dust.
Bless these.   Bless that.
With a blessing that has no fury.

Every Kiss Begins With K-Mart

on a full moon

Your girl flies upstream on precarious feet;
your girl west of the fields, a spotted fawn;
your girl, anagram solver, ironically streaker,
your girl buried in snow under a ponderosa pine,
        three red hearts dealt her;
your girl is something to look at, something that feels;
your girl crushed like a soda can by love;
your girl with a bone in her hand, a curler between her teeth;
your girl still awake at this hour tenuous on the lake;
your girl overcome with green
dark enough to indicate the very beginning of time,
which was when she loved you first,
and your girl, lichens on a spare rock face
becoming one with the other over decades; your girl,
failing to tuck at the appropriate times;
your girl blushing profusely because you looked her in the eye;
your girl, your girl, your girl;
your girl interviewing the late J. Robert Oppenheimer in bed;
your girl in a blue bathroom spiraling into her erogenous center
        and aging like a peach;
your girl taking a bite;
your girl seeing you seeing her and seeing herself
        in your hands like a snake,
the first woman, clay, eternity, whip,
silk, sunset, reeds, silt, clams,

your girl carries herself through the trees,
your girl follows at your heels,
your girl steers you by the arm,
your girl is inside the hotel room bathed in the city's outside
    glow,
your girl is caramel against your lips;
your girl follows you upriver and into the ground;
your girl is between arriving and waiting
in the place birds know best –
your girl dissolves under your tongue;
your girl sleeping in bed next to you like a child;
your girl murmurs in her sleep and turns to you;
your girl tends the water's fall
and at night, transcribes our thunder.

Subs So Fast You'll Freak

Haven't I, in a quarter century,
made too much a mess (unholy) of desire?
Venture out in the strips of trees and bramble
living, fugitives, among the lawns, the ranch houses,
and the light: bats, shriek thin as October's frosts,
racoons yawning from their evening waking.
I am not here made for this gentle lightly world,
not only.   Show me
the undulations, the tenacity and wolfish wiriness
of grey skies. So blooming becomes:
morning sex over the Ohio River & the curling calls
of geese so low they're as much bird as shadow; becomes
laughter brushing up against each other
like waves on friendly cliffs.   Gunshots fade
into the background of our bones. Yes, death desires us.
Time to make the mess holy. Today
I wandered into the weeds of the vacant lot and took your hand.

Brainy

after Czeslaw Milosz

Yes, I do long to be carried like a child
through the trees by something feathery and huge above me,
with wings as long as branches, blocking out the stars.
Think: relations. You can't avoid becoming
eventually. The sound of everyone but you unwrapping
a gift; a child's kidney, a tiny satellite,
the living word.   Patience.   Hostess for the day.
A farmhouse, not lonely, but alone, that single
bright light in yellowed fog that fractures on approach into
    several
lit candles, then returns to one. That fog, old endpapers.
Yes, I do long to be what carries me
and all its hollow bones.
The world ends and no one's selling ketamine.
The world ends and I have my umbrella,
turned inside out by a wind from nowhere.
The gift is a sparrow; the gift is a spark plug
designed to fit just above your left ventricle,
so when you slow down, it reminds you that like it or not,
some birds fall from nests and do not fly.
Some dogs bark at nothing, unsleeping and vigilant against the
    third-shift traffic.
No one believes it is happening now.
Cranes in the marsh. North, northwest. Yes,

I do long to be the starry sky I cannot see, and end the poem
there.
The cloudy dusk-orange of late October indicates
a burning without limit. Appears in daylight's brusque coming-in,
moving past me through the doorway wordless,
though I know for certain what it would say.

So To Speak

When we talk about bloodlines, we mean
chains of continuity.
There are stains
in that house older than any of us.
His replica:
the dismembered
toolbox, unfinished basement,
prone to repetition.

Each child — find the years
and fathers burning off them
as when a lit rag taunts the Cuyahoga
with its nature and says:
I conflagrate.
I conflate you with heavy metals
scraped from the eyes of bloated trout,
mercury simmering, silvering her path
to drown an entire lake. And so become
a line of silvery women without wombs.

Mercy III (Easter)

He couldn't bring himself to say my name. Said he loved me,
always would. Said that he hoped I could come by
for Christmas — *you know how much I like to decorate!* —
and that wasn't it time, really, to return?
I respond with a wartime scrounge.
Get the nails, get the salt. Get the allen wrench and the bread
  knife.
Here are our alternatives.   One: We go with him to open arms.
That leads the way we've come. So what if I write? So what if
  I lie?
A spy can die for her country, and by suicide.
Thus the nails.   Thus the tooth, the cyanide.

On a morning, the bluish world exhumes
every detail, lays the story plain. A girl misled.
A girl squeezed, a lemon to flavor a sea. Nothing left.
And the taste of citrus, the spit of seeds in you.
Nothing could be further from the beach.
Sand bars, out and out. A horseshoe crab's eyes.
See, he was right. There, the body of a young man.
So handsome. Lost weight. Lost waiting for that initial
spark, RNA, lightning, ooze, and glisten. Mouth packed with
  sand.
Look, his perfect, sparkling eyes convince one
death must be the end. And thank goodness.

What punishment could come swift or justly enough
to satisfy?   A lemon squeezed in shot-glass.
Trapped in sand as the tide returns. A Sisyphus of breath.
Get the nails. Get the salt. Get the pinot noir, a fresh hole.
This is where I grew up. Rises, time to time, to grin in open air.
Remember the rot's been with you from the womb.
No flattering white lights glamourize the mire, the bated
clouds and their intentions. I see the body. I see the body.
I know his face. I buried him at sea.

Here are our alternatives. Two: Go with gloves to the other coast,
where we've cleared a space for this last, miniscule sadness,
the one with the mass of a dark star. No shoal. Only beached
    animal made
unrecognizable by bloat. Crawl within the throat.
Cram yourself into a fraught and tightening space.
Outside, the crowd moans. You can't hide forever.
They feel with their palms the movement of the skin pushed aside
by you. Even this space is not yours. Thank you for moments
so near I can smile again.
And fuck you for poems that are duller than the bread knife.
For wasting my time. For being less shelter
to me than the esophagus,
the gullet and the breach. The gloves of an ex's father,
stained richer brown by necessity.

Someone (I won't say who)
taught me dramatics get you nowhere.
You can work for your money
or your money can work for you. The crowd begins to shudder
    and pull apart
the flesh. Slicing thin their palms, barnacles.
My savior is a vermin. My savior is ballooning gas, conceit.
No self to know. No voice to cry suffering. Someone is playing God.

After all.   After none.
Once I fall through, I'm nowhere,
least of all topless at Riis Beach. Father, come meet
the girls!   Look each one of us in the eye
while you try and describe our insufficiencies, our lack.
No words come out. Can all that's left to us
also be glorious? Play around with names. Try one yourself.
We'll decorate you. Nails to the palm, splinter the ligament,
    irreparable
harm. Crown of candles to guide us through the catacombs.
Skull of horse, moonshine, thieves, and justice. Yowl.
Riis beach! Riis beach! Tits out on Riis beach!
        Come to the beach!

Asking permission's for the weak. The beaten.
The bled. I did.   I did. Leeches and all.

I laid the whole story out, tip to tail, filleted it end to end.
Parsed the bones (read a quick fortune)   and offered it up.
Finally they offered me in exchange a slim silver sword
and the chance to become, for a limited time only,
both a simulacrum AND a disappointment.

The crowd bares its teeth. Becomes another
beast entirely. Bless them and their well-informed opinions.
Bless them and their genuine concerns,
their doubts. Bless the light
that fades from stars
years after their real disappearance.
That light comes gorged onto the beach,
chubby and naked and inked. Mr. Leviathan here spit me out.
Father too. Oh, and the body of a son walks again,
or something like that.   These people
and their silly stories!   Next thing you know
they'll say the reward of a life lived to the fullest
is hell itself, and misery comes two-for-one with heaven.

Other Minds

On a morning, earplugs in, the cold so thin
it slides under doors and into mailboxes,
a squid holds tight to my too-fast heart.
Feeding electric.
Take a solvent tab.
Hallucinate exquisite as they are.
Sunlight you with care.
Frail bird. Brief betrayed.
Swing this mood from side til sick.
The wind moves asleep, hormone shift.
Blush to shiver to sweat.
Careful. The squid flutters.
Flakes and varnishes.
Come so north. Come so hearth.
Notice dodges from sight; an eviction slip.
Do the trees imitate.
To me, a yellow house
divided, close enough to wary flood.
To wear a flood. No fire.
No fluctuations to the pulse. Descent
and indecent.
Inciting event passes as steam otherwise, absent.
How many ways can one person torn.
Often shreds. Tattered
and written out, though ciphered.

Swallow them one. And by one let them
shelter below your bed. Then I too run
the same place wind does.

Cordelia

Well may you prosper!

When the sun spoke to us last, it was October,
you had arrived from afar.
When you reconcile this body
teach me what comes next, so I may follow;
you're responsible for both our roses.

I'm in love with you, Cordelia, your head rising above the water,
the smoke rising from your still-lit ring and middle fingers.

Oh, stop. You're just a classical scholar
in love with the image of me,
the fresco of my sainthood on a fraternal wall.

Yes, and?

Further from waves; from the lilacs mad and spreading
like wildfire on this May night. Cordelia lie with me
in the too-cold field, its drowsy sprigs of rain.

Don't listen, let the sound.
Don't touch my lower back,
let the sound
of cars passing on wet roads —

Cordelia, you can't be pinned down.
Your name no longer belongs to you,
the subject, or the object, devoted I.
I'm not attached to freedom.
Nobody holds me down.
I am not the voice, or the light behind my eyes:
I am the fluid chaos of darkness there, Cordelia.
Who but you sees lilacs' madness?

exit left.

Come Along With Me

Covering noise, blanket
over my head, bluewash fleece, and comfort.
No need to see if my eyes are elsewhere.
No need to hear when redirected.
I fear writing soft. I flood writing soft.
Say push me so my back is against the door frame
and single line splits; subduct
that I can only fall so for you.
I'm a habit. Jeans on the floor,
unripe mangoes, luxury communism.
I don't forget fear (I don't regret).
I don't attend galas, I don't reset
over a weekend in the Rockies,
beach yoga, go home for the weekend, liberties,
I stay. I stretch a toe to you, a pinky. I stretch open
a puckered listlessness that woke
only recently from troubled rest.
Don't you see her fleet and ride out into trembling autumn;
furnace sun, infernal cries.
Don't you see her stumble, sleep at peace, draft stories in her head.
And in turn:

cackling in the other room, running commentary to
no-one,
onions on the stovetop, surrounding the cat

with your arms,
stretching your wrist, smiling at me smiling at you,
threading yourself to understanding, a bluish hand,
leftover bakery, your comforting thigh,
no time for tears, happening, happened, will happen:
a new Tang world, game night gin.

With you, something is cooking in the other room,
and someone renamed all the spices for love.

Forgiving Sharon Olds

There are things I've done, that in one world are crimes,
and the other are everyday occurrences.
I doubt my bet, then double down.

On the brink of my first kiss,
I was so hard, so shaken, my head swimming in milk,
hands a frieze in weakness -

Amid that hazy discoordination,
a single car fills up at the gas station
on the strip.

A foal stringy, in the warming hay, survives
long enough for the crystal singe of frost
to creep along the field's edge.

Did I run fast enough?
So fast the thin wires of the cold could reach inside me
and pull out wet coughs like hook-snagged bass?

Leave something in this world you can't live without.
When I kneel on the floor of the bathroom
I am not a sacrifice. Her head swimming in milk.
And it is possible,

desirable, even, to disappear into someone else,
as smoke from a winter chimney dissipates into sky ...
This is determination you see in my eyes, my pledge
to give part of myself away, be remembered, honored,

precious as a strawberry dipped in dark chocolate.
I am so slight and tense with energy
I can run even into the shrouded static of the snowy dark —
a galloping mare becomes steam, flies, and disappears,
        and disappears.

Absolution

I refuse; the absence of action is also an action.
Or so said. Quote me on your book jacket as saying
you shouldn't have said anything at all. Reference me as *et al*
in a paper on girls wet-newspapered by sadnesses.
Ink course through. Black, blue. Rolling on the soil. Where's land?
Her poems over the years became less and less
comprehensible, ambient noise, hero worship, misappropriation.
The problem with exceptional men, their rule.
One to pray, one infest himself with worms,
one reap, one flee far afield.
I refer, of course, to my uncles and their ambitions.
One sister to be brittle, vital as glass. One prayer
to obscure the years. So when I am shredded,
there's no one to point to, and no where.
The lore as simple as a gospel's retelling,
already one deception deep.
Who hurt who, and why. Lo, and behold,
Catholic upbringing (though not mine).
Our prayers for you, daughter, are not the redeeming kind.

Mercy IV

Curled around your feet. Some touch,
some rush towards crosswalk, screech and halt,
only once. Foment. One memory.
Dry calves. Swollen skin around the nails.
They've been in and out all day. When is a need
not . Aperture. Bleary. Symptomatic.
The phone call comes once. Four years now, Theresa,
and not a moment too soon. Fill the sink   and fill
the room and fill the you with water. Soap atolls.
Washing belly.   *Stop writing*
about mercy.

Preen. Shimmer. Not so. Or if so, universal,
Ashbery to Zagajewski. Why must every man.
The leaf pressed between pages. Not even imitate,
even replace. She's found her footing! No more of that!
A lactation pump, a table of sanitized instruments,
room pregnant with incisions.   No one
dying wrongly. Every death labelled
and preserved in a jar. Eco-conscious. Arrythmia
on your chamber door. With an eye toward inclusivity.
Embrace with open. Holy man turned away at door,
scrapped, start fresh-faced tomorrow.

I'm not good at finding the place
where I become a separate entity.
Instead of limits, bargains,
and consolations, may I offer
these words, which I retain
out of loyalty to their original owners,
Greek women about whom
no myths were written — whose poetry
in fragments spells
[

                    ] slender,
and your thighs, which
[
          ] swish, ambitious
[

          ] throughout the path of the sun, we [   ]
can do no more for this world.

December Twenty-Third

for Juniper

What I want to tell you, I can only tell you today.
The wind startling warm and, were it color,
the color of stripped-too-early sapling. Ground ploughed
soft with melting ice casings, drained slate
curtains after sunset.

Trying to catch that green wind
in my hands and wrap it around me like a shawl,
to be ground down, jeans soaked in mud and stained by the
    yellow smudge
of winter grasses.   How exquisite; not exactly
the chiaroscuro violence of a Baroque painting
on a wall across a room of murmurs.

I ask myself what you are asking yourself.
Suspended between contradictions, talk out of both sides of
    my mouth,
promise that this will make it all good.
I will stop lying awake planning to set fire to my father's house,
this time.

And then I am with you.
Oh and how.
        As I brag: with nothing but air
taking tangible shape, as it shapes our lives
into what we longed to be.

I return to earth on days just like this one, neither winter
nor spring,
when no matter how far from my hometown I am
I can smell the sea, and on those days I speak.

Section III. Field Notes and Conclusions

The final year of our study, which saw the subject begin using injections to administer its hormone treatment and added progesterone to its regimen, also saw it decide against the various surgeries available to it through its health insurance. It began using *they/them* as well as *she/her* in public life. It no longer needs to define itself only as a woman. The majority of our team considers this a sign of success — movement away from a femininity that can never belong to the subject toward, at least, an ambiguity that must be further back toward a masculine life.

It must be noted that not all of our team feels that this point is a success. Two of the researchers on the subsection for sexuality, in particular, believe that the subject's involvement in the study and awareness of the experiments being conducted inherently corrupted any conclusions drawn from the project with subjective and inaccurate data. They compared it to a fungus thriving on loam or the ecology of a whalefall. Further investigation connected those researchers to the disgraced X. A. and their conclusions, while important to include as an alternative viewpoint, nevertheless do not deserve to be taken seriously.

More importantly, our patrons have expressed interest in continuing to fund our work with an expanded set of subjects and larger team, as their other avenues of repression have begun to meet resistance from civil liberties organizations and others. We have no doubt that our methods, of disbelief and disapproval, will meet with far greater long-term success.

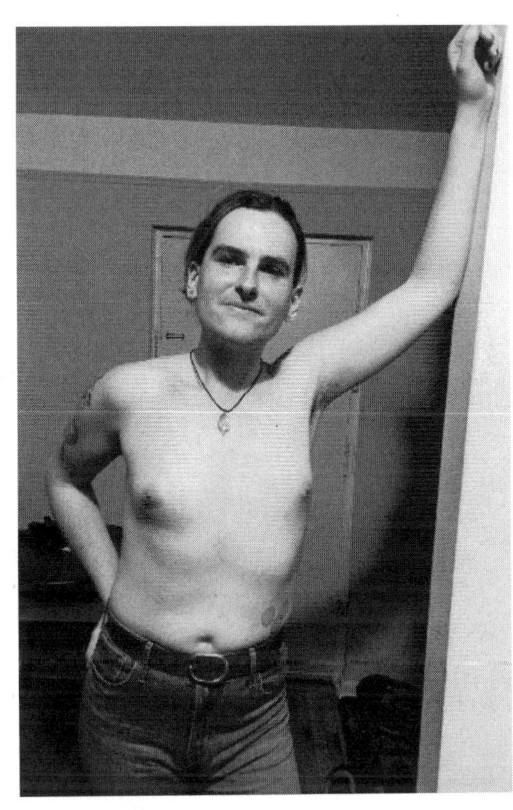

Notes

“White Shirt, Neat Hair” paraphrases Walt Whitman in the line “stay with me and you will know the meaning / of all missing bodies.”

Super-Straight is a self-identification as straight to the exclusion of transgender people of another gender; super-straight men claim not to be attracted to transgender women.

Bruselki: transliteration of the Russian word for “mermaids.”

Suchki: transliteration of the Russian word for “bitches.”

The quote that opens “r/GenderCritical” is from an archived version of the actual Reddit thread.

“bite it, bash it, bruise it:” is a quotation from the Fiona Apple song “I Want You to Love Me.”

“Uwu:” an emoticon depicting a cute face. It is used to express various warm, happy, or affectionate feelings. An “uwu girl” is a girl who brings the emoticon to life through her aesthetic and her demeanor, which tends to be sweetly childlike, but also suggestive, drawing on the sexualization of (usually young) anime girls.

Girldick: a woman's penis.

TIM: an anti-trans slur used by "Gender Critical" feminists; meaning "Trans-Identified Male," referring to a transgender woman.

"Further Excavations" quotes the film *Where the Wild Things Are.*

"Layaway" is written partially in response to Galina Rymbu's poem "My Vagina."

The line about "a dozen letters confirmation" in "Layaway" refers to the laws requiring letters from licensed mental health clinicians in support of Gender Affirmation Surgery in order to schedule a consultation with a surgeon.

"Colossus" refers to the Sylvia Plath poem of the same name, and several other images found in Plath's work and life.

The line "Thucydides / had seven ships   a world to lose," refers to Zbigniew Herbert's poem "Why the Classics."

"Innocents" was inspired by the chapter "Heaven" from Alexander Cheves' memoir, *My Love is a Beast: Confessions.* It also references the video game *Elden Ring,* made by FromSoftware and published by Bandai Namco in 2022.

The title of "A Solitary Feast" refers to a line spoken by Jeffrey Wright's character, Roebuck Wright, in Wes Anderson's *The French Dispatch* (2021).

The line "Someone, I promise, in another time / will remember us ... " is a quotation from Sappho.

"[ ]" paraphrases a line from the Neil Young song "Ambulance Blues" from the album *On the Beach.*

Prior Publications

An earlier version of "Alstroemeria (Thine)" was published in the anthology *The Experiment Will Not Be Bound*, 2022, Unbound Edition Press.

An earlier version of "Layaway" was selected as the runner-up for the 2021 Sappho Prize, and was published online at Palette Poetry in September 2021.

An earlier version of "Subs So Fast You'll Freak" was published in Volume I of *Lean and Loafe.*

An earlier version of "Ballroom Dancing" was published in Issue XII of *The Closed Eye Open.*

Earlier versions of "It Takes Two," "Further Excavations," and "Innocents" appeared in Issue 70 of the *Great River Review*, and were finalists for the 2022 Pink Poetry Prize.

Acknowledgements

My partner Juniper — the home we have made together, and the support and ease we provide one another, have made our years together the happiest of my life. I have seen you grow so much in that time, and you continue to inspire me to work harder and to share more of myself with others.

My beloved Tay — by now, you've heard all of these poems under the light of the moon. You understand so much that I've known all my life, but couldn't say aloud. Let's dream together and share in our devotion for as long as time allows.

My sister, Maddy — for all the reminders to be kind to myself, the poetry critiques, memes, and all we've shared even far apart — thank you, I love you dearly.

My mother — so much has changed in both of our lives over the last few years, and yet our care for one another remains steady. I am so lucky to know someone willing to open themselves to new ideas and perspectives, to humble yourself before what you don't know, and share the wisdom of all your experience. So much of who I am comes from you.

My friend Alex — der andere Teil meiner Seele, eine Zwillingsflamme (sorry, I used Google Translate for that). Your quiet voice and cosmic perspective remind me how to step back and see the stars behind the smoke.

My dear friend and publisher Patrick — while Unbound Edition Press expands beyond your wildest dreams, and you reap the rewards of your hard-earned success, you hold fast to what makes the press great: wildly talented writers and their imaginative, electric work.

My mentor, Peggy — for being such an encouraging, thoughtful supporter of both my creative and academic work. I'm lucky to have found someone who could not only teach me posthuman theory, and guide me through the process of writing my prospectus and dissertation, but also remind me to prioritize my own well-being in an environment where that can too often be secondary.

About the Author

Sophia Anfinn Tonnessen is the author of the poetry collection *Ecologia*, named one of Kirkus Review's Best 100 Indie Titles in 2022. She was the runner-up of the Sappho Prize, a finalist for the Pink Poetry Prize, and was longlisted for the 2022 Industry Prize by *Frontier Poetry*. Her work can be found in *Lean and Loafe, Quarter Press,* and the *Great River Review*. She is a PhD candidate in Slavic Languages and Literatures, and lives in the Midwest with her partner, their cat, and a normal amount of books.

Unbound Edition Press champions honest, original voices. Committed to the power of writers who explore and illuminate the contemporary human condition, we publish collections of poetry, short fiction, and essays. Our publisher and editorial team aim to identify, develop, and defend authors who create thoughtfully challenging work which may not find a home with mainstream publishers. We are guided by a mission to respect and elevate emerging, under-appreciated, and marginalized authors, with a strong commitment to advancing LGBTQ+ and BIPOC voices. We are honored to make meaningful contributions to the literary arts by publishing their work.

unboundedition.com

About the Type and Paper

Designed by Malou Verlomme of the Monotype Studio, Macklin is an elegant, high-contrast typeface. It has been designed purposely for more emotional appeal.

The concept for Macklin began with research on historical material from Britain and Europe dating to the beginning of the 19th century, specifically the work of Vincent Figgins. Verlomme pays respect to Figgins's work with Macklin, but pushes the family to a more contemporary place.

This book is printed on natural Rolland Enviro Book stock. The paper is 100 percent post-consumer sustainable fiber content and is FSC-certified.

Choke was designed by Eleanor Safe and Joseph Floresca.